TRIU
OVER
TROUBLE

TRIUMPH OVER TROUBLE

HUGH F. PYLE

SWORD of the LORD
PUBLISHERS
P.O. BOX 1099, MURFREESBORO, TN 37133

Printed in the United States of America

Table of Contents

Introduction

Everybody has it, but nobody wants it. Trouble!

Someone has said, "Never trouble trouble until trouble troubles you." But most of us have learned that trouble troubles us whether we trouble trouble or not!

"We are troubled on every side," cried the apostle to the Corinthian believers.

"Trouble is near," we read in Psalm 22:11.

"I walk in the midst of trouble," David admitted in Psalm 138:7.

"Man is born unto trouble, as the sparks fly upward," groaned one of Job's comforters (Job 5:7).

Do we know anyone who never has trouble?

A faithful and noble Christian man was indicted on false charges and subjected to years of anguish before a jury declared him totally innocent of all charges. But he had to endure the trouble as his family suffered with him through the ordeal, during which time he lost his job and about two years' pay.

A lovely lady we know had the embarrassing trial of seeing her husband run off with a seductive vixen. He subsequently divorced a wife who had been true to him for so many years.

My son came to see us while his daughters and twelve other young teens were at a summer camp one hundred miles away. At 2:00 a.m. on the morning he was to drive the children back to Pennsylvania he woke up with a terrible pain in his kidney, a pain like he had experienced two years earlier when a stone required surgery. In only a few hours he was to begin a 700-mile journey in a school bus with fourteen young lives depending on him. What could he do?

A grandson, saving to go to college, must have a car to travel to his job. But he found the one he bought was a real lemon that gave him nothing but trouble. What could he do with this trouble?

Newspapers are but a daily report of trouble. And TV news is even worse. We have sympathy for the couple pictured in a cartoon seated at the supper table with the TV set on a stand beside them. She asks, "Shall we watch the six o'clock news and get indigestion or wait up for the ten o'clock news and get insomnia?"

It would not be quite so maddening if these troubles confined themselves to the sinners who "deserved them." But Christians have them, too. Decent, sincere, religious people all have trouble.

Charles Spurgeon said there is a trouble factory inside every one of us; and if we do not get enough from without, we manufacture our own.

What is **your** trouble? Financial? physical? spiritual? material? social?

"What's eatin' on you?" my dad used to ask when one of us boys seemed distressed. He had an uncanny way of spotting trouble.

For years one of the most requested numbers sung by the Old-Fashioned Revival Hour quartet was "We'll Soon Be Done With Troubles and Trials."

An all-time favorite verse when the Bible is quoted is the promise Jesus made in John 14:1, "Let not your heart be troubled . . . ."

A friend said to me, "Why don't you write about trouble?

Help people get out of their trouble, and everyone will buy the book." (I hope he's right!)

Isaiah said, "And they shall look unto the earth; and behold trouble and darkness . . ." (Isa. 8:22). The beloved hymn writer of "What a Friend We Have in Jesus!" asks, "Is there trouble anywhere?" We would have to answer today, "There is trouble *everywhere*."

After twenty-seven years pastoring churches and now another eighteen years ministering as a traveling preacher and writer, I'll have to declare that I have never seen so much trouble. Pastors tell me they have more trouble to deal with than ever before.

God tells us what to do with trouble and—thanks be to Him!—tells us how to get *out* of trouble.

That's what this book is all about.

Hugh Pyle
January, 1993

CHAPTER 1

The Man With Seven Troubles

He shall deliver thee in six troubles: yea, in seven there shall no evil touch thee"—words from the lips of a pious fellow named Eliphaz, one of Job's "comforters" (Job 5:19).

As it turned out, these three fellows didn't know as much about Job as they thought they did. But they were learned in some things; and since all Scripture is given by inspiration of God, we can find some helpful counsel from the Lord in what they said.

Eliphaz promised deliverance from at least seven troubles which he foresaw mankind encountering.

The first (5:20) had to do with *food*: "In famine he shall redeem thee from death."

Many are troubled about rising food prices, and some wonder where the next meal is coming from. There's too much month left over at the end of the money. One woman said she thought she could make both ends meet if she could just get the ends to stand still!

Jesus told us not to worry about food, suggesting that we consider how He feeds the birds of the air. If He can abundantly provide for all of them, can He not most certainly take care of His own dear children who trust in Him?

Years ago I remember hearing about a conversation two of God's birds had:

Said the sparrow to the robin,
 "I would really like to know
Why these anxious human beings
 Rush about and worry so."
Said the robin to the sparrow,
 "Friend, I think that it must be
That they have no Heavenly Father
 Such as cares for you and me."

The second trouble Eliphaz predicted related to *conflicts*:
". . .and in war from the power of the sword" (5:20).

The best of people sometimes have to go to war. And if we are not literally in the army, we still often find ourselves embattled in all sorts of conflicts. As Paul put it, ". . .our flesh had no rest, but we were troubled on every side; without were fightings, within were fears" (II Cor. 7:5). We wage a constant warfare and are enjoined to "fight the good fight of faith."

In this life we will have fightings of one kind or another. Children often face it at school. Workers encounter it in the workplace. Families quarrel in far too many homes.

We have trouble with conflicts—if nothing more than personality clashes.

Tongue trouble is the third kind mentioned by Eliphaz: "Thou shalt be hid from the scourge of the tongue" (vs. 21). In Psalm 31:20, David would be kept "from the strife of tongues."

What the mouth says is a reflection of what is in the heart. Most of us have trouble from talking when we should be listening. Dogs get along better than some people because they wag their tails instead of their tongues.

How many times has my mouth gotten me into trouble! "Why did I say that, when it would have been so much smarter to have said this?" we mutter in retrospect.

Then Eliphaz speaks of destruction and clarifies trouble

number four by resolving our fears of the *beasts* of the earth (vs. 22). People have trouble over their "beasts." The horse that won't trot, the mule that won't pull, the ox in the ditch, were the beast problems of Bible times—and still are sometimes today.

Many go to small claims courts or to "The People's Court," having trouble with their neighbors over the family cat or the dog that barks too much or the stolen parrot or even the parakeet. They encounter "beastly" problems with friends, neighbors or even relatives.

Trouble number five has to do with the *household*: "And thou shalt know that thy tabernacle shall be in peace; and thou shalt visit thy habitation, and shalt not sin" (vs. 24). Sin in the home, family troubles, marriage heartaches—these create BIG trouble for many today.

The sixth trouble described in Job 5 is one relating to *children*: "Thou shalt know also that thy seed shall be great, and thine offspring as the grass of the earth" (vs. 25).

It is impossible to have children and no trouble. G. K. Chesterton said that we spend the first half of our lives fighting with our parents and the last half fighting with our children. Well, thankfully, it doesn't have to be that bad in a Christian home.

All of us have high hopes for our children. We feel that, when they are finally grown, we can rest easy and let them be "on their own." But it isn't always that simple. Many parents find that their heartaches are just then beginning.

They discover that this one felt she/he "married wrong." There is a divorce, and the one comes back to the roost to live with Maw and Paw. Or they don't raise the grandchildren like we think they should. Or they get in a bind financially. Or they stop going to church and end up in trouble.

In some households the troubles seem never to end.

The seventh trouble anticipated by Eliphaz relates to the *end* of life—old age and the grave beyond: "Thou shalt come to thy grave in a full age, like as a shock of corn cometh in in his season" (vs. 26).

How wonderful to know that we can come to the end of life happily knowing that we have done our best, that our faith is in God and we have nothing to fear!

But many come to the end while wrestling with illness, loneliness and anxiety. Senior adults have troubles, too. Sometimes it is with Social Security, Medicare, Blue Cross and pensions. Should we or shouldn't we pay the undertaker ahead of time to bury us? (I have a very difficult time working up any enthusiasm about buying my funeral plot!) What should we leave the children? Can that riotous renegade in the family break the Will?

And, of course, death itself. Are we ready to die? Did the preacher or priest steer us wrong? Can my good works get me in? Or is the Bible really true and we go to Heaven strictly by grace through faith in the finished work of Christ?

How many are troubled at the end of the journey!

These seven troubles are still with us, and they embrace many of the problems and perplexities we grapple with in the last of the twentieth century.

Now as we proceed into the next chapters, we will find out how some have handled their troubles and what to do with yours.

CHAPTER 2

Trouble Comes in All Shapes and Sizes

The Troubles of Job

Job had it all. He is the trouble-man of the Bible. Even people of the world have heard of the trials of Job. James still talks of Job's patience in trouble centuries later (James 5:11). Job originated the saying, "Escaped with the skin of my teeth" (19:20).

If Job could live through and get out of his troubles, anybody can. His house blew away, and his other buildings were demolished in a tornado. His children were all killed. His flocks and herds were destroyed. His wife hollered at him and denounced him. His financial empire was ruined. All this and more. Talk about trouble!

As the drama of this ancient patriarch unfolds, let's take a look at his troubles.

Satan asked God for permission to jump on Job. This came about because Job lived such a good life that God was proud of him and exhibited him as a trophy for Satan to consider (1:8). The Devil was sure that Job was such a good specimen only because God had "hedged" him in with many blessings (vs. 10). Mister Satan thought that, if all of Job's bounty were taken away, Job would curse God to His face (vs. 11).

God, for some reason, gave Satan permission to work Job over. But he had to promise to save his life (2:6).

The rest of these first two chapters of the book of Job tell the sad tale. Job's ranch hands were murdered as his oxen and other stock were stolen by the Sabeans. Next, fire came down, perhaps in a lightning bolt, burned up all the sheep and destroyed the shepherds. Another reporter revealed that the Chaldeans had formed three bands and fallen upon his many camels. The servants, along with the camels, had been slaughtered with swords.

"I only am escaped alone to tell thee" was the sorrowing wail of each reporter.

1. Job's most disastrous blow was when disaster struck his sons and daughters while enjoying a lavish feast at the home of his eldest son.

A Kansas cyclone (or an Alabama tornado) came thundering along and wiped out everything in its path. It smote all four corners of the house where the young people were dining, the house fell in on them, and they all died.

Job arose and rent his mantle. He shaved his head in mourning and fell to the earth to worship God. Then he cried out, ". . . the Lord gave, and the Lord hath taken away; blessed be the name of the Lord."

In all this, "Job sinned not, nor charged God foolishly."

So here we see a good man, a godly man who was living right; yet he had all these terrifying troubles. Satan was the instigator, though we need not suppose that all trouble is from the Devil. But it surely backs up what Peter later wrote—that Satan goes about as a roaring lion seeking whom he may devour.

Job's first big trouble, then, came from the Devil.

2. Next, Job had trouble with physical pain and suffering. In chapter 2 he is smitten with sore boils from head to foot. He sat in the ashes scraping himself with broken pottery. Satan

was sure now that Job would curse God to His face. But patient Job just sat there scraping, scratching, suffering. His faith in God was not shaken.

3. Job's wife now gets in on the act. I have an idea he'd had trouble with her before. She was probably irritated with his pious life.

Sometimes a woman becomes indignant if her husband spends too much time with the Lord or with spiritual matters. Many a man has thrown up his hands and quit serving God when he started getting flack at home. After all, a man wants his home to be a pleasant place. No one wants his/her spouse cutting him/her down all the time. A man knows he won't get much affection from a wife who resents the priorities of his life.

When I was a pastor, a young man surrendered to serve as captain of one of our bus routes. He had not been saved long. His wife made a decision, too, and seemed happy at first.

They enjoyed our church and were excited about all that was going on. But he became more and more anxious to see people saved and to watch his Sunday bus crowd grow. This meant visitation on Saturdays, but she wanted his Saturdays spent with her around their lovely home and spacious yard. She began to press him about it. She would pout and stay home from church.

Soon he slacked up on his bus route. After awhile they weren't coming to the night services. Then he quit his route and later joined a liberal church. Soon they had marital problems and separated.

It is sad when a Christian man has a rebellious wife.

There will also be trouble when a husband does not want his wife to be a consecrated Christian.

So Job's wife figured she would get him to go sour on this religious fanaticism. "Dost thou still retain thine integrity? curse

God, and die," she cried. She had no use for a God who would put her and her family through such devastating sorrow and loss. And she would rather have her husband dead than covered with sore boils and no money left to pay the druggist. If he died, she might at least collect on his insurance.

Job told her off politely but determined not to charge God or "sin with his lips."

4. Economic loss for Job was now evident. His home was gone. His flocks, herds, camels and servants were destroyed. Probably the funeral bills pretty well wiped out what was left. It is never easy to face life when we are up to our necks in financial collapse.

5. Disappointment now swept over Job like a flood. Chapter 3 tells how he cursed the day he was born and wished he had never lived. Now he would rather have died in childbirth, or even before he was born; then he would have been "at rest."

Note that he was in misery and longed for death. He had often feared that he might suffer loss, for now he laments, "For the thing which I greatly feared is come upon me, and that which I was afraid of is come unto me."

6. In addition to disappointment, money, pain and wife problems, Job had trouble sleeping. This is never any fun. No one enjoys lying awake nights, tumbling and tossing. In chapter 7 Job laments, "When I lie down, I say, When shall I arise, and the night be gone? and I am full of tossings to and fro unto the dawning of the day." Insomnia! And to make matters worse, he stayed awake all night long.

Someone reading this may have trouble sleeping. Well, join the club, for multitudes have this kind of trouble. What was Job going to do with this one?

7. Despair added to his troubles now, for he declares that

the days are flying by with no relief in sight and "are spent without hope."

It's really rough when all hope is gone. But life is never completely hopeless for the child of God, and soon Job would find that out.

In chapter 10 we find our hero moaning, "My soul is weary of my life...I will speak in the bitterness of my soul." Are you today in bitterness and despair?

8. Job also had trouble with his sins. We find him crying, "I have sinned; what shall I do unto thee, O thou preserver of men? why hast thou set me as a mark against thee, so that I am a burden to myself?"

Have you ever been so distressed over your sins that you became a burden to yourself? No Christian ever has to go another day under the burden of unconfessed and unforgiven sin. "If we confess our sins, he is faithful and just to forgive us our sins, and to cleanse us from all unrighteousness" (I John 1:9).

Many have trouble with their sins. Come to think of it, I guess all of us have at one time or another. Temptations abound. And about the time we think we have lust and hate conquered, up pop envy, pride and strife. Some men gloat because they have quit drinking beverage alcohol, only to get trapped in the pit of adultery. Another person whips the tobacco habit but has trouble with the sin of foul language.

What kind of sins troubled Job? God thought so much of him that He said that "there is none like him in the earth, a perfect and an upright man, one that feareth God, and escheweth [avoids] evil."

Before it's all over, we'll know what Job's sin was.

9. He also had trouble with his friends. You're not surprised to have trouble with your enemies, but you expect better from your friends.

In chapter 2, Job's three friends "heard of all this evil that was come upon him" and came to "comfort" him. They could hardly recognize poor Job, covered with ashes and boils, sitting in the ruins of what once had been his beautiful estate. ". . . they lifted up their voices, and wept; and they rent every one his mantle, and sprinkled dust upon their heads toward heaven." Somehow I don't think that cheered Job up very much. To make matters worse, they "sat down with him upon the ground seven days and seven nights, and none spake a word unto him."

Sympathetic silence is often appreciated, but they were getting geared up to really work Job over before they departed.

By the time we get to chapter 12 we find Job saying, "No doubt but ye are the people, and wisdom shall die with you." I think by now Job was wishing his friends would go home! In chapter 13 he declared them to be "physicians of no value." And in chapter 16 he groaned, ". . . miserable comforters are ye all. Shall vain words have an end?"

Other friends proved to be not so helpful, too. Concerning these fair weather friends, Job lamented, "My friends scorn me."

To his advisers, his three counselor "friends" who sat on the ground with him, Job finally cried in chapter 19, "How long will ye vex my soul, and break me in pieces with words?" They thought him a hypocrite and were quite certain that he would not have had all this calamity had he not been a secret sinner of some sort.

But that is not always the case. They were worse to him than absolute strangers would have been, for he said, "These ten times have ye reproached me: ye are not ashamed that ye make yourselves strange to me."

Friends mean well, but friends should use good common sense in their comforting.

In chapter 20, one of Job's comforters listed him among those whose "bones are full of the sin of his youth, which shall lie down with him in the dust."

So much for his friends!

10. Job, too, was troubled about death and the fear of the unknown. As he considered the prospects of dying, he sighed, "But man dieth, and wasteth away: yea, man giveth up the ghost, and where is he?" (14:10). Then he brightened a bit as he questioned, "If a man die, shall he live again? all the days of my appointed time will I wait, till my change come."

Job considered death to be "the king of terrors" (18:14).

11. Job also had trouble with the wicked about him. They were anything but helpful. "They have gaped upon me with their mouth; they have smitten me upon the cheek reproachfully; they have gathered themselves together against me" (16:10). Then he continued, "God hath delivered me to the ungodly, and turned me over to the hands of the wicked. I was at ease, but he hath broken me asunder: he hath also taken me by my neck, and shaken me to pieces, and set me up for his mark."

Job, the tormented one, became "a byword of the people" (17:6).

12. He even felt that he had trouble with *God*, for in 19:6 he exclaimed, "Know now that God hath overthrown me, and compassed me with his net." It is too bad when we get so troubled that we think even God is against us.

13. Finally, we learn that Job's troubles were compounded by misunderstanding. In chapter 30 he laments that the commoners had him in derision. The town folks turned against him, he felt. The young people, who had admired and envied Job, now felt that he must be some strange kind of person so to incur the wrath of the Almighty.

Job said, "And now am I their song, yea, I am their byword.

They abhor me, they flee from me, and spare not to spit in my face." It is very troublesome to be despised and misunderstood. Poor Job!

Now what was the solution? What did he *do* about all this? How did he get out of his great trouble?

We must note that his cure was progressive. Gradually he reaped the benefit of it all and began to see God's plan in it all. Someone has well said that those who see God's hand in everything can best leave everything in God's hand.

There was going to be a happy conclusion in all of this—as there will be in our troubles, too, if we learn to trust God to solve them for us.

In the midst of his worst fears and pain, Job shouted, "Though he slay me, yet will I trust in him" (13:15). He made up his mind that God was going to see him through his calamity and that he would believe God if it killed him!

It dawned upon him that, since he had learned (14:1) that man is born unto trouble, he was certainly not alone in his predicament. That always helps.

Next, in chapter 16 he learned that his troubles would not last forever: "When a few years are come, then I shall go the way whence I shall not return." Since our life here "is even a vapour, that appeareth for a little time, and then vanisheth away" (James 4:14), we know there will soon be an end to our misery.

Purity is something else he learned through his trials. ". . . he that hath clean hands shall be stronger and stronger" (17:9). "I shall come forth as gold," he prophesied in 23:10.

The Lord also became very much alive to Job through his troubles, and he caught a glimpse of the Saviour in the famous exclamation, "For I know that my redeemer liveth" (19:25).

How often has the Lord become more precious to me

because of the difficulties that threw me totally upon Him!

A great man of God wrote a book, *Crowded to Christ*, and that's just what God was doing in Job's life.

In chapter 21, he was taught what happens to the wicked who are not fortunate enough to experience the purifying process of God's loving favor: They "become old, yea, are mighty in power." Their farm animals even seem to get along better. Their children dance and learn to play instruments as "they spend their days in wealth." But they grow up godless, with no thought of the Almighty. They are soon thrust into eternity, and often in a violent manner.

So the wicked are not to be envied.

The Word of God has become so meaningful to Job now that he loves it "more than my necessary food" (23:12), and his heart is getting soft and warm toward the things of God.

Suffering hostages have testified to the power and blessing of even a fragment of Scripture recalled from childhood and scribbled on a paper bag, when they were being subjected to trials and pain.

But isn't it too bad that often we wait until pain strikes to fall in love with the Bible?

Job now finds the Word richer and tastier than his necessary food.

He admits in 24:22 that "no man is sure of life." Or, as David put it, ". . . there is but a step between me and death" (I Sam. 20:3). This helps us to appreciate every day of life He allows us to have.

Our hero gets a glimpse of God's great power in 26:7 as he learns that our Heavenly Father is the One who stretches out the North over the empty place and actually hangs the earth upon nothing. A God who does that can certainly take care of our puny troubles.

He comes close to the wisdom of Solomon when in 28:28 he declares, ". . .the fear of the Lord, that is wisdom; and to depart from evil is understanding." Next, in 29:20 he exclaims, "My glory was fresh in me," and in chapter 31 he makes a covenant with God about his eyes, acknowledging that God counts "all of my steps."

Weaned From Covetousness

In chapter 31 it seems that Job is realizing that he has had his mind and eyes too much on money and was making gold his hope and confidence.

Pastors have told me that, even in Christian schools today, most teens have set their sights on a career and money-making rather than a ministry for Christ. Usually they are following in the steps of their parents. The love of money is still "the root of all evil." How we need to teach our little ones that material possessions are not the truly important things of life.

Job admitted that he had been guilty of rejoicing because his wealth was so great. One of God's warnings is, "If riches increase, set not your heart upon them" (Ps. 62:10).

One of the sublime truths of Scripture is unveiled for Job and us: "For he will not lay upon man more than right" (34:23). This is great consolation in trouble—He knows how much we can bear. "When he giveth quietness, who then can make trouble?" Elihu uttered these words, but Job learned them and recorded them for us.

Songs in the Night

He has found songs in the night composed by his Maker (35:10), and this is so much better than the "trouble at midnight" (34:20). Only the trusting believer can sing in the darkest night of trouble.

Job learns from Elihu in chapter 36 that it pays to serve the

Lord and that, if we obey Him, we'll spend our years in pleasures. Job's original three mourning "comforters" had flunked the course, but God did send along this Elihu who, even though he did not fully understand Job, nevertheless made some sympathetic and sustaining statements that helped not only Job but all of us who have troubles.

Our hero is now beginning to see "the bright light which is in the clouds" (37:21); and finally in chapter 42 this "troubled man" learns that God can do anything! He is brought to the end of himself as he utters these words, "I have heard of thee by the hearing of the ear: but now mine eye seeth thee. Wherefore I abhor myself, and repent in dust and ashes."

God then turned the captivity of Job and called upon him to pray for his "comforter" friends who had judged him so harshly. Here God gives Job twice as much as he had before! People began to bring him money and jewelry as his friends gathered around again, along with his brothers and sisters.

One wonders where his brothers and sisters were when he really needed them. But God sometimes lets us be shut up to Him to learn valuable lessons that can only be taught in the valley of the shadows.

God gave Job seven more sons and three more daughters, and these daughters were the fairest in the land. He lived an additional 140 years.

So we come to the end of the famous trials of Job.

Our troubles do come to an end.

CHAPTER 3

Where Troubles Originate

You can start out on a beautiful spring day without a care in the world, and be up to your neck in trouble before time for the coffee break.

Where do all of these troubles come from?

It's easiest to blame them on the Devil. But some of my troubles I cannot rightly charge to "his majesty."

Suppose I run out of gas six blocks from the office. The Devil didn't do that. I just kept forgetting to fill the tank.

Or old Joe gets stopped for speeding and finds himself in trouble with the county Mountie. Can he blame God or the Devil for it, when it was his foot that was heavy on the pedal?

Or maybe you back over the neighbor child's toy wagon. You're in trouble because you now feel obligated to pay for it. But at least you rejoice that the neighbor kid wasn't in the wagon at the time!

As in the case of Job, the man from Uz, troubles can mount up and descend in large quantities upon our respective heads. Where do they originate? Well, what does *God* say about it?

1. They often are caused by *people*. "Lord, how are they increased that trouble me! many are they that rise up against me," David cried in Psalm 3:1. A lot of our troubles are people troubles—if neighbors were just not so ornery, if in-laws

not so nosey, if children not so rebellious, if teachers were not so demanding, if bosses were more understanding.

2. Troubles may come from our enemies. Those who dislike us just may not be above deliberately causing us trouble.

At this very time a most malicious book has appeared on the market defaming the name of the wife of a popular former president. Many who knew her well declare that the book is full of lies and made-up trash. Yet the book is overnight becoming a best seller. The lady is in trouble not of her own choosing. Even if she is innocent, many revel in such gossip.

Friends say she has been attacked by those who didn't like her to begin with.

The same is often true of slanderous lies that are told on good and successful preachers.

Troubles often come from our enemies. But a person who has no enemies isn't generally doing much that's worth disturbing the Devil about. "What did I do wrong that yonder villain praised me just now?" is a quote from Spurgeon.

In Psalm 13:4 we find David saying, ". . . lest mine enemy say, I have prevailed against him; and those that trouble me rejoice when I am moved." Enemies who want us to move may devise means of troubling us so we will!

3. The *flesh*—our old carnal nature—is often responsible for our troubles. In urging people to use great caution when considering marriage, Paul warned about possible "trouble in the flesh." "The works of the flesh" can lead us into all sorts of trouble. "I know that in me (that is, in my flesh,) dwelleth no good thing. . . ," Paul reminds us.

4. *Cults* and heretics will trouble us. Satan, of course, is behind this; for he is the author of confusion and hates the truth of God's Word. ". . . there be some that TROUBLE you, and would pervert the gospel of Christ" (Gal. 1:7). And again,

". . . certain which went out from us have troubled you with words, subverting your souls. . .," declared James in Acts 15:24. Heretics abound today.

5. *Money* and prosperity often are a source of our troubles. Proverbs 15:16 teaches us, "Better is little with the fear of the Lord than great treasure and trouble therewith." Most people soon discover that wealth does not bring an absence of trouble—just a greater variety of them!

6. *Evil spirits* will, and sometimes do, trouble us. When the Spirit of the Lord departed from Saul, "an evil spirit from the Lord troubled him."

Evil spirits are demonic spirits, but God can control them, use them, subdue them or remove them. He also allows us to reap bitter consequences if we persist in disobedience, as Saul did. And God may dispatch one of these evil beings to teach us that we reap what we sow.

7. *Things* can trouble us, if we are not careful. ". . . thou art careful and troubled about many things," Jesus told Martha (Luke 10:41). God is able to "give good things to them that ask him," we are assured in Matthew 7:11, so why do we get so disturbed and troubled about things? God knows what things we have need of before we even ask, the Word teaches.

8. Trouble comes, too, from our own *evil hearts*. Jeremiah 17:9 shocks polite society with its condemnation of all hearts—every human heart—as being "deceitful above all things and desperately wicked." Isaiah said, "The wicked are like the troubled sea," and because of this trouble on the inside, "There is no peace, saith my God, to the wicked" (Isa. 57:20,21).

This heart is the trouble factory Spurgeon told about.

9. *Rebellion* against the Word of God, too, will bring trouble upon us. Psalm 107 speaks of those who "rebelled against the words of God, and contemned [scorned] the counsel of

the most High." So He brought down their hearts with labor, causing them to fall down and find they were without help. "Then they cried unto the Lord in their trouble, and he saved them out of their distresses."

It pays to behave and obey the Bible if we want to escape such trouble.

In my pastorates I have known good people who nevertheless were worldly in mind and did not want to hear what God said about sin, judgment and retribution. In their rebellion against truth, they joined a church where they didn't have to hear Bible preaching. Soon they were in trouble of one kind or another.

10. *Standing* for God and righteousness may land us in trouble. God never said it would be an easy road—this path of discipleship. "A man's foes shall be they of his own household," Jesus warned. "Yea, and all that will live godly in Christ Jesus shall suffer persecution," promised Paul.

The book of Acts is a record of the troubles as well as the triumphs early Christians encountered because of their faith and stand for God.

Paul expected trouble because of his stand and would have been surprised if troubles, conflicts and distresses had not come his way. In II Timothy 2, the "soldier" chapter, he speaks of the glorious truth of the resurrection of Christ, then continues, "Wherein I suffer trouble, as an evil doer, even unto bonds."

So if we live a positive and powerful Christian life, we will stir up devilish opposition and scorn from the unsaved and even from some carnal Christians.

Trouble!

These are just some of the sources of trouble. Do not think that as a believer you will be immune.

CHAPTER 4

When Trouble Overwhelms Us

"We are troubled on every side," the grand apostle said in II Corinthians 4:8. If they came just one at a time and then gave us time to recuperate, it wouldn't be so bad. But they often come in pairs, or in triplicate. Or with some of us, it seems we're kin to Job, and troubles deluge us!

A couple we know are devoted and consecrated Christians, yet they have recently suffered a flood-tide of trouble until I'm sure they feel like Jacob when he cried, ". . . all these things are against me."

The husband has gone through a very severe testing with his business, causing him to lose a very good paying position. Now in his new work one problem after another has arisen, causing a postponement of funds for many months. One deal after another has been complicated by difficulties, held up or canceled.

They have had personal problems, business trials, financial setbacks until I'm sure they could have cried out, "We are troubled on every side."

They sold their boat and a fine custom van to lighten the load. They have been ignored by "friends" they would have just sworn would have stood by them in their distress.

Now as they look back, they have learned who their true

friends are. God gave them wonderful peace through the storm, and they feel God may have allowed all of this not only to strengthen their own faith but to fortify their children as well. The daughters have grown spiritually through it all and were privileged to witness God's mighty power in answering prayer.

God brought them through with flying colors.

A dear pastor friend, a fervent soul winner, has been betrayed by an associate he befriended. The church is a strong church with a great missionary program. Satan hates the work, of course, and has inspired the associate to siphon off unsuspecting people and turn them against their good pastor. Physical illness has aggravated the pastor's heartache over the matter.

Many churches—often highly successful churches—suffer in similar fashion. Of course this is the very kind of work the Devil wants to destroy. Never have good churches been under such attack.

It will be interesting to see how God works this one out.

A lovely high school senior was the chaplain of her graduating class and a witnessing Christian. A nice shore holiday was planned for her, with several of her friends, after graduation. But disaster struck when she realized some of her friends were trying to induce the others to do things she knew a Christian shouldn't be involved in. When some of them were sent home, the others decided to leave, too. So the long anticipated party was a great disappointment.

Children can have their troubles, too.

One of our granddaughters went to a youth camp last summer but came down with a virus on the first night. She had to stay in the infirmary most of the week and couldn't enjoy the food for which her parents had paid one hundred dollars.

Her older sister was engaged to be married and developed bronchitis just as her showers and other festivities began.

Fortunately, with care and prayer, both girls were soon well again. Troubles don't last forever.

Last fall my wife and I started out in our motor home on our fall preaching mission with no idea how much trouble we would encounter. The first week it was an electrical wiring problem. Next, we left the step down and bent it out of shape against a log while backing up. Then the door lock jammed on us, and we couldn't get the main door open from the inside. We finally had it replaced to the tune of about $100.00. Next, we found our carpets were getting wet, so we had to call in the plumber for the leaks.

Our worst day was when the water pump conked out as we traveled. It was Saturday, and we had 250 miles more to go to our next meeting. We spent eight hours in high weeds by the roadside while a dear Christian mechanic wrestled with our problem. It seemed most everything else had to come out of and off of the engine to get to that water pump! It took time to find the mechanic, then the parts; and he didn't have the tools and equipment we would have had in a repair garage. We couldn't get to any food. After we got on the Interstate, we were soon overheating and had to stop again to replace a thermostat.

At the next church we had to have some tire work done. And we found the bushings on the stabilizers were shot. When we left that church on a windy morning in a driving rain, my wife had been up most of the night with a stomach virus. We had nearly 800 miles to drive to our next appointment.

And some people think the traveling life is a ball!

Yet God brought us through all of those troublesome events and sent us just the person we needed to help us in each case. He answered prayer for my wife, and she was almost well when we arrived at the last church on our itinerary. The sun came out. The Lord wonderfully blessed in those meetings.

To top it off, He impressed my heart to hunt for a new motor home last Christmas. We couldn't afford to do this, but He led us to a wonderful vehicle with only a few hundred miles on it. Then He impressed some interested Christian friends to help us pay for it!

You just can't beat the blessing of the Lord!

So overwhelming troubles are not always so bad after all. Not for the child of God.

We live in a sin-cursed society where Christ is rejected and God is blasphemed. The Bible is a joke to the entertainment industry. Black snow falls morally.

So troubles overwhelm the race. We see it on the news each night. A CBS news correspondent said recently that there are some forty places on the globe where some kind of military conflict rages. And that doesn't include the streets of cities like Washington, Atlanta, New York and Miami after dark.

America sinks in a sea of booze. Prisons groan with over-crowding. "Crime Runs Wild" was the recent headline in a news magazine. We don't know what to do with our garbage. The ozone is breaking up. AIDS has become epidemic. Tanning is dangerous. Something is wrong with almost everything we eat. Yes, man is "of few days, and full of trouble."

The experts don't know what to do, but they keep trying to outguess one another. It was Vance Havner who said, if all the experts were laid end to end, they would never reach a conclusion.

We will never solve the problems of the world until we solve the problems of the individual. Man's great malady is sin. The heart of the problem is the problem of the heart—"deceitful. . .and desperately wicked."

Which brings us back to you and me. Can we survive the troubles that seem to overwhelm us? Better still, can we be triumphant when everything around us seems to collapse? I'm sure that we *can* even if, as David put it, "The troubles of my heart are enlarged" (Ps. 25:17). In the midst of troubles, the child of God can hear His voice, "Let not your heart be troubled."

When I was a young Christian, a visiting singer taught us a song I've always remembered about the way you "carry the load." It went:

> **Put your burden on your back;**
> **Never put it on your heart:**
> **It's the way that you carry the load.**

The psalmist writes of "great and sore troubles" which God had shown him. Why did a man after God's own heart have to endure such overwhelming trouble? Well, for one thing, we wouldn't have had most of the book of Psalms if he hadn't! "For whom the Lord loveth he chasteneth" (Heb. 12:6). Chastening is not always punishment. The word also means to purify, to refine.

So after David spoke of the "great and sore troubles," the sweet singer of Israel triumphantly exclaimed, "Thou shalt increase my greatness, and comfort me on every side." With victory like that, who minds a little trouble?

Job came out of his overwhelming troubles "as gold," while Peter assures us that trials are much more precious than gold. So all things do "work together for good" to the obedient child of God. Our troubles are not in vain even when they seem to be overwhelming.

The three Hebrew children had even more influence after their experience in the burning fiery furnace.

> **When the Hebrew children in the fiery furnace lit;**
> **They just smiled and praised the Lord**
> **And didn't burn a bit.**

So hang on.
Help is on the way!

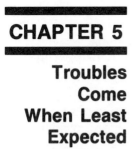

CHAPTER 5

Troubles Come When Least Expected

Fire broke out in an Atlanta skyscraper recently. One commentator remarked about how those office workers left home Friday morning looking forward to the weekend with anticipation. But four died in the flames and smoke that day. One lady jumped six stories and is hospitalized in critical condition. Many others were injured or suffered smoke inhalation. No one expected the electrical explosion that caused the tragedy. How quickly trouble can change the entire format of our lives! Help came quickly and most survived.

My wife and I travel to most of our appointments in a 33-foot motor home. For several months with one vehicle we had a series of difficulties with the distributor as the rotor cap kept burning out. When this happened, our apartment on wheels would die a sudden death, and I could only steer for the shoulder of the road and signal for help.

This happened once during a storm, and we could just barely get off the pavement. Big tractor trailer rigs roared by and shook us violently. I had a hard time finding a wrecker that could tow us in. When I did, this fine "deacon" (he said) really took us in, in more ways than one! People think about the glamour of travel, but they don't think about the trouble.

We've had bolts slip out of the alternator brace and hit the fan blade (very unnerving), tires bubble up and send us scur-rying for new ones, fuel filters clog and bring us to a chug-ging, sputtering halt, and alternators fail us in the most inconve-nient places.

Once the ignition system caught fire and blazed up under my feet as we traveled down a lonely gravel road in the back country. My wife learned how to use a fire extinguisher in a hurry.

On a steep incline in the wilds of Wyoming, we failed to start at all and had to use our CB to summon help. With one motor home, the copper tubing kept breaking, which meant wet, cold, soaking carpets under our feet.

The power generator has shorted out, leaving us baking in 100 degree heat. (When we're on the road, the air conditioners don't work without the generator.)

In our last motor home, the furnace never worked when it was cold, and we didn't need it when it was warm. Again and again we had it worked on. It would be purring like a kitten when we drove out of the shop. But when we got up into a colder state, out she went!

So preachers and other Christians have trouble, and it usually comes when least expected. It is not a disease for sinners only.

Job said, "For the thing which I greatly feared is come upon me. . .I was not in safety, neither had I rest, neither was I quiet; yet trouble came" (3:25,26).

When Saul picked up the throne of Israel, he didn't know the trouble he would have with the Amalekites.

Jonah certainly didn't anticipate his submarine trip in the interior of a whale when he booked passage on that ship to Tarshish. But he had plenty of trouble when the storm raged and they tossed him out into "whale's belly chapel."

When Esther became queen, she had no idea of the trouble she and her people would encounter.

Could Ruth and Naomi ever have imagined that they would become lonely widows when they stood happily at the marriage altar?

Trouble at Midnight

Elihu declared that "the people shall be troubled at midnight" (Job 34:20). It's too bad when trouble strikes at the midnight hour. We can stand most anything when the sun is shining bright. How much easier trouble seems then! But at midnight?

Paul and Silas endured the earthquake at midnight. Surely they didn't need that on top of imprisonment in the Philippian jail. They had been beaten. Their backs were bruised and bloody. Their heads were aching. They no doubt wondered why God permitted all this trouble. But in reality it was the earthquake that brought their deliverance.

There's a lot of trouble going on at midnight. Ask the local police. Talk to the emergency room crew. Check out the fire department. City newspapers keep a staff working all night to cover the trouble at midnight. This is true partly because men are sinners and love darkness rather than light, because their deeds are evil (John 3:19).

So God sent the earthquake at midnight for Paul and Silas. And as a bonus, the jailer and his family found salvation! God knows what is going on. And how good it is to live in a civilized country where the police and fire specialists can take care of much of the trouble at midnight while we sleep.

But we will all have our midnight hours.

Yesterday the doctor gave me a bit of alarming news following a medical checkup. A verse in Job came to my mind: "What? shall we receive good at the hand of God, and shall we not receive evil?" (2:10).

I thought upon all the good things God has brought us recently and reflected on the words of the blessed hymn I love that tells us to count our blessings and name them one by one. Somehow I just couldn't conjure up a worry to save my life, so I turned it all over to the Lord and slept like a babe last night. It will be most interesting to see how my Heavenly Father will take care of this matter.

Troubles come when least expected. Ezekiel had no idea that his wife would have to die as a sign to Israel (Ezek. 24:16-18). Moses did not realize he would have to spend forty years with the sand and sheep of Midian on the back side of the desert to be used of God. Elijah did not foresee the wrath of Jezebel when he stood valiantly for God on Mount Carmel (I Kings 17,18). We all have our unexpected midnight hours.

"I die daily," Paul said, never knowing what the next day would bring. In Isaiah 17:14 we read, "And behold at eveningtide trouble." The day is done. It is time for repose, but "behold, trouble!" Trouble not only comes at night and in the morning but in the eveningtide.

The phone rings, and often it is trouble. If it happens after bedtime, you can almost always know it is! I was even relieved once to get a call from a drunk who was trying to dial Buster's Bar. It was so late at night, I almost knew the call spelled trouble. So even a wrong number may turn out to be a blessing.

Now look back at some of the troubles of Bible people mentioned earlier in this chapter. Esther had trouble, but God used her to deliver her people from destruction.

Ruth and Naomi found provisions, love and even wealth after their trouble in Moab.

Paul and Silas were triumphant at Philippi.

Moses, Elijah and Paul came through their troubles with flying colors.

But we'll all have our "midnight" trials in this world where "man is born unto trouble as the sparks fly upward." Since unexpected troubles will come at any moment, wouldn't it be wise to have a contract with God ahead of time that we're going to trust Him to guide and deliver? He is the only One who can truly help us.

You may not have any trouble at all just now, but the Bible says that "trouble is near" (Ps. 22:11).

Will there be someone to help?

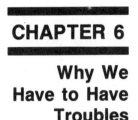

CHAPTER 6

Why We Have to Have Troubles

"I walk in the midst of trouble...," David declared in Psalm 138:7. But he didn't stop there: "Thou wilt revive me: thou shalt stretch forth thine hand against the wrath of mine enemies, and thy right hand shall save me." Out of the depths of his troubles David saw there was hope, help and salvation. So the trouble turned out not to be so bad after all.

"The troubles of my heart are enlarged," he cried in Psalm 25:17. Sometimes they get bigger before they disappear. God wants us to come to the end of ourselves and realize that He is our way out of difficulty.

Do your troubles seem to "enlarge" today?

If There Were None

Can you imagine what life would be like if there were never any kind of trouble at all? What would the fire department do if we never had fires? If no home had plumbing problems, the poor plumber would be out of a job. If there were no emergencies, what would the emergency crews do with their time? If no one got sick or had accidents, the hospital people would have to change vocations.

If you work in an insurance office, you are profiting considerably by the fact that people have trouble. Banks are supposedly making our money problems simpler. The TV repairman would go hungry if no one ever had trouble with the set. And what about the auto mechanics?

But need we go on? What does the Bible teach about why we have to have troubles?

1. To learn that the Lord is good. Nahum 1:7 reads, "The Lord is good, a strong hold in the day of trouble; and he knoweth them that trust in him." Just as a little child is apt to snuggle up to and enjoy the embrace of his mother even more when he is in trouble, so we know that God seems nearer and dearer when trouble has arrived.

"As one whom his mother comforteth, so will I comfort you," God says in Isaiah 66:13. How very sweet!

I remember the first church where I conducted a revival meeting. A man came with regularity to the meetings and was enthusiastic about the preaching. He had a fine family. He was a real help to that pastor. "But it hasn't always been that way," he told me. "That man moved here from up North and settled in with next to nothing. He came to church and was eager to learn. He struck it rich in celery. God blessed his farm, and he got so busy, he dropped out of the night services. Then he got too busy to come on Sunday mornings. So God let him get wiped out. His crops failed. His equipment broke down. His children gave him trouble. He had to bury his parents.

"So then as a 'poor boy' again he sheepishly came back to church with his family. He has made a comeback in more ways than one. He is a happy, busy, witnessing Christian once more."

That man learned of the goodness of the Lord through his troubles.

2. To make God's house more meaningful. David said some things during his troubles that found him paying his vows to the Lord when the troubles had ceased (Psalm 66). Then he declares, "I will offer unto thee burnt sacrifices of fatlings, with

the incense of rams; I will offer bullocks with goats. Selah [Think of that]."

David is here bringing his sacrificial offerings to God, but it appears he must have been slack about it until his troubles drove him back to where he belonged.

We don't need to bring animal sacrifices to God as the Old Testament saints did. But perhaps it is money or service or time we have been neglecting. Trouble is a good reminder of our failings.

David had a sharper testimony for God after his troubles. In this psalm he is happily exclaiming, "Come and hear, all ye that fear God, and I will declare what he hath done for my soul."

Through it all he had learned, "If I regard iniquity [sin] in my heart, the Lord will not hear me." Was the trouble not worthwhile? Many a person has come meekly back to church to renew his acquaintance with God after trials and tears had worked him over.

3. To quiet and settle us in our faith. In the midst of prosperity it is easy to get too busy, too excited or too popular for our own good. Job said, after his calamities came, "I was not in safety [his wealth only made him *feel* secure], neither had I rest [was he too busy making money to rest in the Lord?], neither was I quiet [he stayed in a dither], yet trouble came" (3:26).

The glitter and sparkle of the world might ruin us if we did not have trouble to subdue us before Him. Many a man or woman has "simmered down" when a heart attack came along. Suddenly they found they had plenty of time for God and for quiet meditation, after all.

In Job 23:14,16 he is found saying, "For he performeth the thing that is appointed for me. . . . For God maketh my heart soft, and the Almighty troubleth me." "And to you who are troubled rest with us. . . " (II Thess. 1:7).

4. To save us from covetousness. "He that is greedy of gain troubleth his own house" (Prov. 15:27). Many a woman with credit card mania has had to tear up the cards because of the troubles that came with her spending sprees. "Things" can get to us. Someone said that men used to ride chargers—now they marry them!

But hold on! Men may be guilty of this, too, and sometimes are even more likely to squander money on sports, outdoor equipment and pleasures while neglecting things that are really needed in the home. This makes for trouble.

"A man's life consisteth not in the abundance of things," the Saviour taught. God will give "good things" to them that ask, if we will walk simply before Him and trust Him.

On the other hand, "He that troubleth his own house shall inherit the wind" (Prov. 11:29). Grasping, covetous people may soon be "gone with the wind" of adversity.

5. To strengthen and perfect us. First Peter 5:10 says that, "after that ye have suffered a while," the God of all grace will "make you perfect, stablish, strengthen, settle you." God wants us strong. He wants us to bear testimony to the poor, pitiful world around us. He is also preparing us for Heaven. We are being conformed to the image of His Son (Rom. 8:29).

So He frequently allows us to have troubles to strengthen and perfect us.

All of us know people who have come through great trials and troubles only to become mature, exemplary and fruitful Christians. Thus, "the trial of our faith" is "much more precious than gold" (I Pet. 1:7). Troubles can make or break us. A loving God would have us profit from them.

So He declares that all things work together for good to them who love the Lord. And, "If we suffer, we shall also reign with him" (II Tim. 2:12). Learn to value your troubles. For as Job learned, " . . . when he hath tried me, I shall come forth as gold" (23:10).

CHAPTER 7

Is God Concerned With Our Troubles?

Does Jesus care when my heart is pained
  Too deeply for mirth and song;
As the burdens press and the cares distress,
  And the way grows weary and long?

Oh, yes, He cares; I know He cares,
  His heart is touched with my grief;
When the days are weary, the long nights dreary,
  I know my Saviour cares.

—Frank E. Graeff

God says in Psalm 50:15, "Call upon me in the day of trouble: I will deliver thee, and thou shalt glorify me." So Jesus cares. God IS concerned with our troubles.

In Psalm 81:7 God reminded His people that they had called and He had delivered them "in the secret place of thunder" as He proved them "at the waters of Meribah." So God is aware of our troubles and will deliver us in His own way, at His own time.

Sometimes it is in the secret place of thunder that God shares His secrets with us, so we can expect often to find His help in and through the storms. Obviously, we should cherish our tempests and trials.

God says here that He proved the children of Israel at the waters of Meribah. Meribah means "strife." It was the spot where they "strove with the Lord" about water, getting Moses so agitated that he angrily smote the rock twice (Num. 20:11).

The Lord is, indeed, concerned about our troubles but sometimes has to allow them to test us for our own good.

It seems at times that God is hiding His face from us when we have trouble. David once cried, "Why standest thou afar off, O Lord? why hidest thou thyself in times of trouble?" (Ps. 10:1). Yet David went on to find that the Lord was with him even in the valley of the shadow of death.

So cheer up, troubled reader. God is alive, all-powerful and very much aware of the burdens we bear and the troubles that terrify us. Our Heavenly Father promises, "He shall call upon me, and I will answer him: I will be with him in trouble; I will deliver him, and honour him" (Ps. 91:15). God has been with me and honored me even when I felt I deserved it the least.

". . .the salvation of the righteous is of the Lord; he is their strength in the time of trouble" (Ps. 37:39). There we have it again. He is concerned about the troubles of the righteous. And the righteous are those who have been *made* righteous through faith in the finished work of Christ.

The skeptic can sneer. The wicked can wallow in his wrath and wantonness. But the child of God knows by experience that the Lord is concerned with our troubles and is looking after those who are looking unto Him!

Finding this to be so, Paul penned these words about the God of all comfort, ". . .who comforteth us in all our tribulation, that we may be able to comfort them which are in any trouble, by the comfort wherewith we ourselves are comforted of God" (II Cor. 1:4). So He comforts us sometimes to make us comforters and not just to make us comfortable.

He wants believers to comfort and help those around us who are in trouble. People would be more anxious to come to the God of all comfort if they saw that we were letting God get us out of the troubles we get into. When believers use the same tactics and tricks as the unsaved world, it is no wonder they have no confidence in our God!

"When he giveth quietness, who then can make trouble?" (Job 34:29). "There is a place of quiet rest, near to the heart of God," the songwriter reminds us.

As we travel across America, hardly a week goes by without some Christians telling us how God has brought them out of trouble. Why do millions of people keep going back to church every Sunday—and many of them three times or more a week? If they had not learned that God is concerned about them, they would have given that habit up long ago!

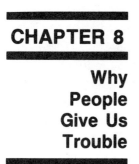

CHAPTER 8

Why People Give Us Trouble

The cynic who said, "The more I am around people, the more I appreciate my old dog," has many a sympathizer. Why are some people so troublesome? It does seem like members of the human race should be able to get along. Much of our trouble is *people* trouble.

If you have trouble at work, very likely people cause it. And most family troubles are problems with people. Jealousy, greed, malice, envy, anger, strife, selfishness—these problems create people trouble.

Daniel had trouble with the Chaldeans after Belshazzar was slain. The new king, Darius, promoted Daniel to a place of honor. And he was "preferred above the presidents and princes, because an excellent spirit was in him" (Dan. 6:3). But the other officers were obviously jealous of Daniel and "sought to find occasion" against him. Daniel had more trouble with them than with the lions!

Moses had his troubles with the people of Israel who, when the going got tough, wondered why they ever followed him out of Egypt.

Cain was upset with his righteous brother Abel and ended up killing him. He was certainly not the last of relatives who resent the spirituality of some other member of the family.

Jesus said that a man's foes shall be they of his own household.

Our own loved ones sometimes seem to be the last to understand us when we make full commitment to Christ. Jesus' own brethren in the flesh did not believe Him. So are we surprised if all our loved ones do not understand our spiritual battles and conquests?

A little boy said, "My great grandfather fought with Napoleon, my grandfather fought with the French, and my father fought with the Americans." His young friend replied, "Your people couldn't get along with anybody, could they?"

Well, when we live out and out for Christ, it does seem sometimes nobody can get along with us, no matter how hard we try to get along with them!

Jesus said, "If the world hate you, ye know that it hated me before it hated you" (John 15:18). So we should not be surprised when we have trouble with people.

Paul wrote, "From henceforth let no man trouble me: for I bear in my body the marks of the Lord Jesus" (Gal. 6:17). Paul had had enough trouble from men. He bore the marks of human suffering in his own body. He had been whipped, stoned and mistreated in many other ways. He suffered most at the hands of people. So will we if we are what we ought to be. "All that will live godly in Christ Jesus shall suffer persecution" (II Tim. 3:12).

The saintly and faithful Joseph in the Old Testament had brother troubles. They were jealous and sold him into slavery.

Elijah had his biggest troubles with people. He got along fine with God. He was fed by ravens. He could part the waters of Jordan, ascend to Heaven in a chariot of fire. But he surely had his troubles with the Baal worshipers and the devotees of Queen Jezebel.

So it goes through the Bible. It is a Book of people in and out of trouble.

Now why do people give us so much trouble? Let me cite a few reasons:

1. " . . . the flesh is weak" (Matt. 26:41). People often plan to do better, for "The spirit indeed is willing." But we have a fallen human nature, and even Christians, if we do not earnestly "watch and pray," will fall into temptation and a snare. Unless we put on the whole armor of God, we will be in for a first-class battle with the flesh. The flesh—our frail human nature—is greatly influenced by our moods, our physical infirmities and our personality quirks.

God knows the weakness of our flesh, for we read in Psalm 103:14, "For he knoweth our frame; he remembereth that we are dust."

2. Stunted maturity. One has said, "You are only young once, but you can stay immature indefinitely." People who should have grown up long ago still act like babes. A young bride pouts, cries and runs home to mother; but if she is that immature, she was not old enough to get married in the first place. Young men think they are smart, brave and in command; but when the trials of marriage come along, they may storm, swear and bluster like a spoiled brat. So there is trouble.

Christians should "grow up into him in all things" (Eph. 4:15). Paul tells us to "grow in grace," but many saints never take that seriously. Preachers feed the people first on the milk of the Word, then try to give them "strong meat," only to lament that many of their members never grow spiritually but remain "babes in Christ."

3. Disposition and personality clashes. Take a good look at sour, grumpy people: often they come from a family of that disposition. Some folk seem to have been weaned on a vinegar bottle.

Like father, like son. Many a woman is said to be the "spitting image" of her mother. Of course, the grace of God should remedy a lot of this, and frequently does. If such sour saints would really obey the command of Ephesians 5:18, to "be filled with the Spirit," it would make all the difference in the world. We need to become transformed into the likeness of Christ.

Sadly, most of us know very few Spirit-filled saints.

To further complicate things many of our problems are with the unsaved. Many can be very troublesome. Some are even proud of their cantankerous ways. You wonder if they were vaccinated with lemon juice. Why can't everyone be sweet like you and me?

Personalities differ. We might as well expect it and allow for that. Even though we're all cut out of the same human mold, "some are a little moldier than others!"

A fine black preacher I know started a church in a "converted" massage parlor. "I rub some of them the wrong way," he laughs. Don't we all? I rub some people the wrong way without even opening my mouth. I had to learn a long time ago that I could never please everybody and it was foolish to try.

And there are some people you'd hate to be shut up with very long.

Some we enjoy being with more than others. You just "hit it off." They seem to understand you. It may be cultural, academic or psychological; but often our disagreements are just personality clashes that could happen to anybody.

4. Financial anxieties contribute to people difficulties. "Money makes the mare go," but money can make the fur fly, too. Money can get us into mighty touchy situations.

That person who snaps at you in the office may have been

just faced with a stack of unpaid bills. The other fellow may have some debts that would stagger you. So we need to be patient with those who are troublesome—we have not yet walked in their shoes.

The lady who "lost a fortune in the market" may have had her grocery bags break and spill in the corner store! Her children may be hitting her up for new designer shoes.

Maybe that man who was short with you didn't get the raise he wanted. Or his wife is wearing out the plastic with his MasterCard. He and she may have had a row that morning; now he is taking it out on you.

One girl said, "Money must grow on trees, or banks wouldn't have so many branches." My dad used to remind his boys that money didn't grow in the backyard.

A farmer said he hoped his hens would never learn what bricklayers received for laying bricks. Many people stay in a constant dither about money.

Dealing with the unsaved will be different from confronting the troubles of fellow Christians. (In the last chapters of this book, we give some help for such troubles, financial and otherwise.)

CHAPTER 9

When Trouble Hits Home

Where we should have the least trouble, many have the most! Home should be a haven of rest and relaxation. Around our own loved ones we ought to be able to be calm and collected. "Home, sweet home," is what people long for. Many have fond memories of home, while others have memories not so fond.

Home troubles consist of husband-and-wife disagreements, parent-and-child conflicts, sibling rivalry, arguments over money, in-laws, illnesses, responsibilities, discipline, meals, and a hundred other things.

"In sickness and in health" is part of the wedding vow at most marriage ceremonies. Yet many marriages begin to crumble and break up when one or the other comes down with something.

"There's a plague in the house" was the cry in the home of the leprosy-stricken Israelite in Leviticus 14. And there's many a "plague" smiting the homes of people today. When strong drink is tolerated or gambling tickets or pornographic materials or violent videos or illegal drugs are allowed, you may be sure there is a plague in the house!

"In the house of the righteous is much treasure; but in the revenues of the wicked is trouble" (Prov. 15:6). How true!

When money squabbles develop, how wise to read on in Proverbs 15:16, "Better is little with the fear of the Lord than great treasure and trouble therewith."

King Solomon, who had homes, wives and money, knew what it was to have trouble.

Many worldlings stop off at the bar for a "bracer" so they can face what they have to see and hear at home. Many can't stand to leave home, while others take the first opportunity.

One southern worker said, "I don't know what my wife does all day, but I do wish when I got home the oven would be as hot as the TV set."

A hotel received a call from a traveling man who wanted to know if they had a room where he could put up with his wife.

I read where the Helping Hand Society enjoyed a swap social. Every lady brought something she no longer needed. Many of the ladies were accompanied by their husbands!

Police found a man throwing big rocks at his wife while she was drowning in a Pennsylvania river. But he explained, "I was just trying to drive her back to shore."

Most young couples have never stopped to realize all of the problems, pains and perplexities they will encounter when they try to live together under one roof. Much of what God tells us through the wise king in the book of Proverbs has to do with solving the problems and troubles of the home.

Many a man is his own worst enemy at home. Proverbs 11:29 reads, "He that troubleth his own house shall inherit the wind." So some husbands and fathers create their own storms. Police will tell you that a great portion of their calls are to stop domestic fights that have erupted in the home.

I have written a little booklet called *Keeping the Honey in the Honeymoon.* One preacher told me that, after his wife read it, she got so sweet that he almost had to run from her! He probably exaggerated, but it's amazing how many good Christians allow themselves to forget the little things that keep trouble at a minimum in the home.

Pastors have me come for several days or for a week just to preach and teach on the home and marriage. We have met in plush hotels, at rustic campgrounds, in church auditoriums, to talk about the heartthrobs and heartaches of the home.

Recently I was in a family life conference near the Virginia coast. During the meetings we had the biggest snowstorm of the decade. I managed to slush and slide my way back to the motel, then over to the church again the next morning; but I was sure the crowd that early Saturday would be pitiful in weather like that. Imagine my surprise and delight to find an even bigger crowd than the day before, and almost as many as we had at night. Young couples were hungry to find out how to make their homes happier, how to reduce tensions and troubles they constantly encountered.

In an earlier pastorate, a young husband taught his wife how to handle and fire a gun. A few short years later she fired the gun—at *him*, and he dropped dead. I never knew exactly how much of that disaster he may have brought upon himself.

A Harris Poll revealed that what people want most in life is a good family and a happy home. We each have a tendency to blame someone else when the home goes sour. "The woman whom thou gavest to be with me," Adam cried when God asked him what went wrong and who had enticed him to eat of the forbidden fruit.

When I was a teenager, and later as a young husband, there were many lovely and romantic love songs floating through the air. Every time we turned on the radio we could hear such tunes as "The Very Thought of You," "The Nearness of You," "Goodnight, Sweetheart," "The Touch of Your Lips," "I Love

You Truly," "As Time Goes By," and "I'll Be Seeing You." Whatever happened to songs like that? You could almost fall in love just listening!

I feel sorry for young people today when so many songs have just a "beat" instead of a tune. It sounds more like murder and machinery than magnolias and melody. No wonder there's so much terror and trouble in the home today.

Well, in a little bit we'll see if we can find a cure for whatever it is that has happened to the modern home. We don't have to have such trouble in paradise.

CHAPTER 10

Trouble With Sickness and Health

"Stay healthy," we're constantly told in the medical and financial announcements and reports of the day.

"Don't Get Sick" was the title of a recent *Parade Magazine* article. Looking at the skyrocketing cost of medical care, we conclude we can't afford to be sick!

But how do we avoid such trouble?

When I was a pastor, so many of my calls were sick calls. And getting so many of them, doctors had to stop making house calls. Every other newscast or talk show has advice on staying well, much of it contradicting what you just heard on some other program!

Is there anything left that we can eat? Remember the cranberry sauce scare a few years back?

Then when the big hullabaloo over sugar came, we switched to artificial sweeteners. Then when we were informed they were dangerous and might cause cancer, down came the ax again.

We switched to honey, only to be informed that was not much better than sugar. Out West a man gave me a huge box of chocolate candy while at the same time informing me that chocolate was what was killing people in this country.

We are told now to use no sugar nor sweeteners nor cream nor milk substitutes in our coffee. (I always liked a little "false doctoring" in mine.) But not to worry, for some "experts" now say we shouldn't be drinking coffee either!

So we switch to tea, only to be told there's almost as much caffeine in that.

Then they tell us that if we drink hot chocolate we're getting a bad combination of chocolate, sugar and milk. Milk is suspect, anyway, since cows eat grass that has been sprinkled with acid rain.

Cold drinks and beverages are off-limits because of caffeine and sugar. Switch to apple juice, then along comes the warning about insecticides that may have penetrated the apple's skin.

Health authorities have always told us to eat lots of vegetables—but now the bug sprays and preservatives used on them may be dangerous. If you try to grow your own, the bugs gobble them up. Then again, there's the acid rain.

That leaves us with fruit. Once more you have the problem of chemicals, not to mention the citrus blight in Florida and the poisoned grapes in South America.

We are urged to leave off all dairy products, so there goes our cheese and other milk and cream delights. America loves ice cream, but that must go, too. Cookies have white flour and sugar in them. That goes for cake and pie, too.

Ham has always been a big issue, and now they're jumping on red beef, too. Fat and cholesterol put the fast food places on the "hit" list, so they install salad bars. Next, we learn that these salads are sprayed with something to make them stay fresh longer.

Chicken seems to be our best bet, and then the salmonella scare comes along. Something fowl here!

So we switch to fish. Surely fish will be safe and healthful. But many waters are polluted, we learn, and the fish have been affected. Same thing for shrimp and other shellfish; and of course there's the cholesterol again.

Well, we're down to nuts. Squirrels seem to thrive on them. But, alas, they have cholesterol, too. So there goes my peanut butter, I suppose.

This leaves us with oat bran, which they're putting in everything. How long will it be before we hear that bran is injurious to our health?

Since we are frail humans at best, there will always be health problems. Mankind is under a curse because of human sin. So we are all dying a little bit every day. But most of us could last a lot longer than we do with a little common sense. It is, indeed, a fact that people are living to be older and millions of us are staying healthier than ever before in history. We can learn something from all this.

Staying healthy is easier than getting sick and having to get well again. Medical treatment is expensive. It is no fun to be sick. Much of today's trouble has to do with medicine, doctors and hospitals. The further we can stay from these, the better. *Parade* states that by the year 2000, only 4100 of the 6800 United States hospitals will still be in existence. Thirty-one million Americans have no health insurance whatever. Because of malpractice insurance, very few doctors will even consider delivering a baby. And older Americans are informed that the roadside health clinics may not always be safe places to go.

So How to Survive?

How can we feel good, stay healthy and avoid health troubles? The Bible advises "moderation" (Phil. 4:5). Most doctors agree that moderation in matters of diet, exercise, rest and medication is the best policy.

From our own experience and from observation in the ministry for decades, may I make a few vital suggestions? These things have worked for us for over fifty years of a happy marriage and a fruitful ministry.

For breakfast we enjoy one egg every other day with only a

small amount of crisp bacon from which all the grease is dried off—this, along with whole wheat toast, orange juice or grapefruit, margarine instead of butter, and a small amount of homemade jam. Coffee and tea are used in moderation and usually with only a small amount of sugar or sweetener and low-fat milk.

The other mornings we enjoy bran cereal, juices, fruit, and wheat toast.

Using a little honey makes it unnecessary to add much of the other sweeteners. Reducing the amount of sugar and taking smaller servings of desserts satisfies the old sweet tooth while being obedient to the law of moderation.

When we do splurge and cook steaks, we buy the leaner and smaller ones. Fresh fish, properly prepared, can be just as tasty as shrimp and without the cholesterol. Taking the skin off the chicken before you eat it eliminates most of the fat. Use baked potatoes instead of fries. Rice is a good alternative. Try chicken baked instead of fried for a wholesome change.

We use plenty of fresh salads daily as well as cooked vegetables, so we don't need big meat servings. Taking smaller bites of meat makes more room for vegetables. Try it. It is now believed broccoli and cauliflower help to prevent cancer. If you don't like carrots, try them thinly shaved in your salads. They are colorful and delicious this way. It is believed that sprouts and some seeds are good for you, so they can be included in a tossed salad. Celery and onions add zest and flavor, according to taste. Go easy on the creamy dressings if you tend to have a problem with cholesterol.

Avoid the caffeine drinks at night, and you may find yourself sleeping better. It is best not to let the children get the habit of swilling cola drinks and gobbling sweets. Good health habits can easily be taught to them while they're young, and you will save troubles with sickness later on in life. Learn to enjoy fruit juices. They are delicious, especially if you can get them fresh.

We drink only distilled water unless we can get well water we are reasonably sure of. Use pure water and drink plenty of it. On this most doctors agree.

Get enough sleep. Seven to eight hours of sound, restful sleep is adequate for most people. Some find they can get along on less and still feel good all day. Some find they can get by on a little less at night if they can work in even a brief nap in the afternoon.

Keep Active

More and more health authorities advise exercise in moderation for good body tone and general well being. I personally feel so much better if I get in that brisk walk and other exercises almost every day of the week. Brisk walking is excellent. I sometimes jog for a block or two, then fall back into the fast walk. Rope-skipping, bicycling and swimming are good alternatives. Stretching and sitting-up exercises help to keep one limber and get rid of the "kinks."

I enjoy mountain-climbing (in moderation) and wood-chopping, as well as other outdoor activities. Tennis is good exercise and doesn't kill a whole afternoon as, for instance, golf does.

Most of the above can be enjoyed by people of all ages, as I have certainly proven! Keep it up with regularity, and this enjoyment can be yours even to a ripe old age.

Tobacco and Booze

Every doctor and medical authority we know of now urges people not to use tobacco in any form. The terrible blow to health caused by smoking and other tobacco forms is well known—the injury to lungs, heart—in fact, the whole body. Cancer experts believe smoking kills more people than any one thing in America today.

People who have quit tobacco testify to the immediate

change in their physical well-being. A friend of ours who quit after forty years of puffing said he could actually taste his food again for the first time in years. He told me he had not been able to run or even walk fast. And going upstairs almost did him in. Now he wakes up feeling great, does not have that awful ashtray taste, can walk fast, hurry upstairs, and even jog without discomfort. This, along with being able to taste his food again, has made a new man out of him.

My booklet, *How to Quit Smoking Without Pills, Pain or Panic,* has helped many people to easily kick the habit.

Smokeless tobacco, such as chewing tobacco and snuff, also keeps many people sick. Teenage boys, who think it smart to chew like their sports idols, are developing cancer of the mouth, throat and tongue.

Drinking alcoholic beverages has put millions in institutions and millions more in an early grave. Talk about trouble! The drinker is asking for it. Hospitals groan with the victims of booze. Beer usually leads to the drinking of the hard stuff. All wine saps do not grow on apple trees. Those who say they "can take it or leave it alone" usually take it every time.

"Wine is a mocker, strong drink is raging: and whosoever is deceived thereby is not wise," wrote Solomon in his wonderful Proverbs (20:1). "At the last it biteth like a serpent, and stingeth like an adder" (23:32).

So that's what the Almighty thinks about booze in any form. Alcohol was made for rubbing and other external uses, not to pickle our interiors. Leave it up to human depravity to figure out a way to destroy the body in the name of enjoyment.

Attitude and Disposition

It is a fact that the disposition has much to do with health. This is why Christians who really believe the Bible and trust in the Lord can go through desperate circumstances without breaking under the pressure. "Thou wilt keep him in perfect peace whose mind is stayed on thee: because he trusteth in thee," wrote the eloquent prophet in Isaiah 26:3. Then in the next verse he continues, ". . . in the Lord Jehovah is everlasting strength."

"A merry heart doeth good like a medicine," exclaimed Solomon in Proverbs 17:22. Previously, the great king had found a wonderful contrast in Proverbs 15:13, "A merry heart maketh a cheerful countenance: but by sorrow of the heart the spirit is broken." He goes on to say in verse 15 that the merry heart has "a continual feast."

We should always maintain our sense of humor, learn to laugh at ourselves, practice the wearing of a smile and roll with the punches when things seem to go wrong. God will help us with this if we will let Him. We all have different personalities, but most of us can improve our dispositions with the Lord's help.

"My meditation of him shall be sweet," David cried joyfully in Psalm 104:34: "I will be glad in the Lord." We have the Lord, so we can be glad even when things go amiss. David accomplished much of this by singing to the Lord, he explains in verse 33.

Have you tried singing to the Lord? I can't sing, but I can carry a tune. I love music, and I find myself constantly humming or singing to myself the beautiful words of grand old hymns and gospel choruses that I've known and loved since childhood. Try it!

With determination, faith in God, and a bit of will-power, most of us can avoid much of the trouble many have with their health.

To top it off: PRAY for your own health and that of your loved ones every day. John set a good example of this in III John 2. For many of us, this may be the way of escape from such troubles.

CHAPTER 11

Trouble at School

Young people have troubles, too. And often these are centered around activities at school, whether on the local scene or away on a distant campus.

God's counsel from the Bible will surely work as well here as in any other place. If students will learn certain principles about mastering trouble, they will be happier now, and it can save them a lot of grief in the business and social world later on.

Consider some of the problems that may lead to trouble at school:

1. Peer pressure. Far too many students are extremely concerned about what other students may entice them or urge them to do.

2. Covetousness. Many find themselves chafing over the talents, possessions, luxuries or advantages other students have. This, in turn, may lead to the temptation to let down their standards.

3. Popularity. Some students let themselves become so anxious to be popular that they get into trouble trying to impress the crowd.

4. Laziness may well keep a student from getting organized in his room, or it may lead to poor grades because he or she fails to buckle down and study.

5. Selfishness. Many students have trouble at school because they do not truly consider the feelings and wishes of room-mates. There has to be give and take.

6. Troubles. Prejudiced teachers build resentment or animosi-ty in students because of a certain bias or because they are sometimes unfair, especially to a Christian student who has standards and principles they strongly believe in. Of course this brings trouble.

7. Activism, "rights," and issues. Sometimes one is brand-ed one way or another even if he tries to remain neutral in such matters.

8. Dating someone who appeals to you may backfire and turn to trouble unless you are certain of the character, background and disposition of that one before you start dating.

Now there are no general solutions to campus problems, but these are some of the trouble spots. And the student can usually avoid trouble if he or she is fortified with faith and is aware of our resources.

Try this: At the very outset, before you are ever tempted with peer pressure, make up your mind that you are going to be your own person. Ask God for the grace and wisdom to make you a rugged individualist before the first temptations ever come. Remember this: what God and your parents and true friends think of you is much more important than what the student body thinks of you.

Thank God for what you have rather than worrying about what you don't have. Develop your own talents. We are all different. That person you envy may be miserable. Perhaps he would give anything to have the peace God has given you. So set your own goals and follow through.

Popularity with the crowd is not nearly as important as hav-ing a clear conscience, a few real friends, and the joy of achievement. Establish your own standards before temptation strikes.

You can cure laziness. Get yourself by the knap of the neck and make yourself get organized. Read a manual on the subject or get help from someone who is organized if you can't figure out how to do it yourself. Study from the very beginning; then you will not get behind and have trouble catching up or passing tests.

Whether in the classroom or dormitory, there will always be the possibility of clashes because of personality conflicts. Some are just harder to get along with than others. Many have never been taught manners. One person is emotional and high-strung; another is not. But it is a proven fact that kindness, thoughtfulness and unselfishness pay off in a big way.

Selfishness is a sin. Confess it to God and renounce it. Then practice thinking of others. Try seeing how nice you can be. You'll be amazed at how much better you'll be liked. And you will like yourself better in the process!

You cannot always do anything about domineering and prejudiced teachers, but you can pray for them, be nice to them and purpose to prove by your actions that you have something in your character that they need, too. Even if you never change them one bit, you will have strengthened your own faith and inspired others.

Regarding issues, you cannot always remain neutral. Just be sure the matter is worthy of your time and energy. If it is a matter of morals and values, take your stand firmly and "do right if the stars fall," to quote another.

Dating problems are, of course, worthy of another book. Again, what your character and your own standards are before you leave home will have a lot to do with whether you fall into compromise in the area of dating. Get acquainted around other people and in broad daylight before actually agreeing to date. Ball games, school productions or concerts, academic lectures, and especially church services, are good places to start friendships and dating activities.

It is far easier to avoid dating troubles than to get out of them.

Christian students are His witnesses in one of the greatest of all mission fields—the pagan school campus.

"But Daniel purposed in his heart that he would not defile himself with the portion of the king's meat, nor with the wine which he drank" (Dan. 1:8). His mind had already been made up before the temptation came.

"Let no man despise thy youth; but be thou an example of the believers," the great apostle challenges us in I Timothy 4:12.

This kind of student will probably not be the most popular one on campus, but the friends you have will be for real. You'll have a clear conscience, and God will be pleased with your life.

Furthermore, you'll save yourself a lot of trouble!

CHAPTER 12

When Trouble Goes to Church

Unfortunately, you cannot escape trouble by attending or joining a church.

Many times people are disillusioned because they felt the church to be a refuge from trouble. But we cannot hide in the church and be sure we'll never have trouble again.

A church in Atlanta was totally demolished in a devastating tornado last week. More than once in the last couple of years robbers have rushed into churches, holding the congregation at gunpoint while the parishioners were stripped of their wallets and jewelry.

When I was a pastor, we once had purses stolen from the choir room while the owners were singing in the choir!

But these are not the only troubles faithful Christians may encounter when they go to church.

First, no matter what kind of burdens or troubles believers have, let me assure you that it is still best to be a Christian.

And very likely the Christian who goes to a Bible-believing, evangelistic church will run into more difficulty than if he or she went to a cold, formalistic or liberal church. If the Devil already has it pretty well frozen into place, then he does not need to extend himself in a church where they're not doing him very much damage anyway!

Satan in the Sanctuary

When Peter warned of the Devil going about like a roaring lion to see whom he could devour, he was singling out Christians as the targets.

When Paul warned of "trouble in the flesh," he had believers in mind, as he did when he warned of troubles on every side.

It was to the saints at Galatia—and today—that he told about religious cultists who would be engineered by Satan to trouble us.

It was in the Temple of God that the money-changers ran into trouble—with the Saviour Himself!

Peter didn't know it, but the Devil himself had gotten into him when he heard the rebuke of Christ, "Get thee behind me, Satan."

So don't be surprised if you run into Mister Satan in the sanctuary as well as in the street or shop.

Why Trouble at Church?

When peace is declared with the Lord, then war is declared with the Devil. Satan will be most anxious to discourage, if not destroy, those who most diligently serve the Lord.

Not only with Satan but with the flesh will we sometimes have trouble. Self dies hard. The flesh does not like to be ignored, much less crucified. The old self-life has a mean habit of coming down from the cross!

In addition to the flesh and the Devil, the world will give us trouble. It fascinates, then assassinates. This world certainly is no friend to the child of God. Jesus reminds us, "If the world hate you, ye know that it hated me before it hated you" (John 15:18). The servant is not greater than his Lord. When we identify with the Lord, we make trouble with the enemy of the Lord. James reminds us that "the friendship of the world is enmity with God."

Again, our deceitful hearts can play tricks on us. When Jeremiah speaks of this, he reminds us that the heart is "desperately wicked." This may explain why Christians can get cross and belligerent toward one another, each feeling that he is in the will of God in so doing. God tells us we should "be of the same mind one toward another," and, "Be not wise in our own conceits" (Rom. 12:16). We often get into trouble with fellow believers without even realizing who is pulling the strings.

Satan can start a dirty rumor among Christians and inspire some saints to repeat it. Or we can devise some scheme and get into serious trouble, as Ananias and Sapphira did, forgetting that "covetousness is idolatry" (Acts 5:1-10; Eph. 5:5). Neither knew he or she was making his or her own funeral arrangements that day!

One would have to become familiar with the entire New Testament to know how to handle all the trouble that can develop in a church. Hence the need to soak in the Word of God and let its precious truths become part and parcel of our very being.

Preachers find there can be as many troubles as there are people in a congregation. So they need to pray for the wisdom of Solomon, the patience of Job, the courage of Daniel, the boldness of Elijah, the purity of Joseph, the meekness of Moses, the vocabulary of Isaiah, the compassion of John, and the power of Paul.

Personality clashes, stubbornness, pride and carnality—all combine and conspire to make for trouble in the church. When you add the determination of Satan to wreck everything God designs to do, you can readily understand how easy it is for troubles to arise.

To avoid such trouble is most desirable. For this, we need

to let the Word of Christ dwell in us richly in all wisdom. We also need to pray earnestly for ourselves and for one another. We certainly need to obey the command of Ephesians 5:18, "Be filled with the Spirit."

In order for all of this to be effective, we must die to ourselves and be crucified with Christ (Gal. 2:20).

Paul gave us a wonderful formula when he said, "Walk in the Spirit, and ye shall not fulfil the lust of the flesh" (Gal. 5:16). Otherwise, we will need his warning in the previous verse. ". . . if ye bite and devour one another, take heed that ye be not consumed one of another."

In my book, *What Every Preacher Should Know*, I have a whole chapter on "Facing, Solving and Avoiding Problems"; and there is another chapter on questions and answers for pastors who hope to avoid troubles in the ministry.

Meanwhile, all Christians need the solid equipment of "the whole armour of God" to withstand "the wiles of the devil" (Eph. 6:11).

CHAPTER 13

What to Do With Your Troubles

Since we all have troubles, what is the solution? What does God teach about how to get out of trouble? What do we do with our troubles?

Sometimes we best find out what to do by first knowing what *not* to do.

1. Unfaithful men will fail us. Before we share our trouble with men, we had better be absolutely sure they are qualified to help. A bankrupt man is hardly the one to give financial advice. God put it this way: "Confidence in an unfaithful man in time of trouble is like a broken tooth, and a foot out of joint" (Prov. 25:19). We will hardly be helped with our burden by nursing a bad tooth or by hobbling through our calamity on a crippled foot.

Neighbors, fellow workers, friends and even family members may be quick to offer a solution; but often they are themselves "unfaithful" comforters who have more sympathy than sense.

King David had a wayward son named Amnon who fell into flaming temptation. In his frustration he had a friend who gave him a very bad piece of advice which resulted in the crime of incest, and that led to his death at the hands of his cruel brother Absalom.

> The arm of flesh will fail you—
> Ye dare not trust your own.

2. Satanic sources can be a tragic risk. King Saul got so far away from God that he consulted the witch of Endor. He was full of fear and jealousy, sensing that David would soon be king. To his servants he gave the command, "Seek me a woman that hath a familiar spirit, that I may go to her, and enquire of her" (I Sam. 28:7).

Saul knew better than to do this. He had formerly given the order to cut off from the land wizards and fortune-tellers. Now he gives in and goes to one himself.

Deuteronomy 18 warns us about witches, astrologers, enchanters, charmers, necromancers and such. In chapter 13 of the same book, God again speaks of "prophets" and dreamers of dreams who give signs and wonders. We learn in this chapter that such were to be put to death in those days under the law.

Those fascinated by the New Age movement thus need to beware! It is the old satanic trickery back in a new dress.

In Galatians 5:20 "witchcraft" is listed as a work of the flesh right along with adultery, fornication, uncleanness, idolatry, hatred, murders and drunkenness.

So the way out of trouble is never to be found here.

3. We find no solution to our problems in our own hearts. Solomon wrote, "He that trusteth in his own heart is a fool . . ." (Prov. 28:26).

Jeremiah 17:9 says, "The heart is deceitful above all things, and desperately wicked"; so the heart is an untrustworthy guide.

How many times have we heard someone say, "I just feel in my heart that it is the right thing," even though discussing something the Bible expressly forbids. When I was a pastor, a young woman said to me, "I know he's not a Christian, but my heart tells me to marry him anyway." She had been tricked by a deceitful heart to disobey the plain command of God and marry an unbeliever.

A businessman I knew felt he could trust a young man who had recently made a profession of faith after coming out of a life of known sin. He took him into partnership without really finding out much about his previous dealings. Soon my friend found he had been swindled out of a substantial amount of money, and it took him years to recover. He almost lost his entire business because he sincerely believed that the fellow could be trusted.

The heart is not always a reliable guide.

4. Neither is money the panacea for all of our troubles. In this present money-mad society it is believed by many that, if they can just get their hands on enough money, everything will work out fine. But money can fail, as the people found out in Egypt during the great famine described in the days of Joseph. "When money failed . . . in the land of Canaan," they "came unto Joseph, and said, Give us bread: for why should we die in thy presence? for the money faileth" (Gen. 47:15).

People who had counted on the stability of their favorite Savings and Loan organizations in the past few months have found that money can fail.

Movie, TV and rock stars are among the wealthiest of all people; yet the rate of suicides, drunken debauches and drug overdoses is among the very highest with these people. So money fails to bring the happiness and satisfaction it promises. We cannot count on it to keep us out of trouble or get us out of trouble.

A fine and intelligent businessman in Florida has just been charged with first-degree murder and faces life in prison for murdering two people while under the influence of drink and drugs. He has now found Christ, but his substantial reservoir of wealth cannot set him free nor bring him back to the fine position he once held in our state.

So what DO we do with our troubles? What is the answer to the question, "How do you get out of trouble and stay out?"

David cried, "Give us help from trouble: for vain is the help of man" (Ps. 60:11).

Many of us remember the popular old gospel song, "Where Could I Go but to the Lord?"

Has it ever crossed our minds that those who wrote such songs found the solution to the trouble problem—songs that begin, "I have found a hiding place when sore distressed," or "I've anchored my soul in the haven of rest"? What about, "There's no disappointment in Heaven," "I've discovered the way of gladness," or "Since Jesus came into my heart"? It sounds like these hymn writers knew something about escape from trouble—temporal and eternal.

The Gulf War in the Middle East was won by the USA and our allies. Much prayer went up for our fighting forces. A Southern Baptist chaplain said he believes God placed "a hedge of protection" around allied soldiers in this war and that "the low casualty rate was His miracle." I agree.

After the advent of the atomic bomb in the forties, we were urged to prepare underground survival shelters in our backyards. A few people did. One happy old saint in a testimony meeting said, "Psalm 91 is my bombproof shelter." In time of war, many Christians have read and believed that chapter. Read a few verses from it:

"I will say of the Lord, He is my refuge and my fortress: my God; in him will I trust. . . . He shall cover thee. . . under his wings shalt thou trust: his truth shall be thy shield and buckler. Thou shalt not be afraid for the terror by night; nor for the arrow that flieth by day. . . . For he shall give his angels charge over thee, to keep thee in all thy ways."

How to Get Out of Trouble

1. Know that God is most anxious to help. In Psalm 91:14 God speaks of the one who has set his love upon the Lord and has known His name; then immediately He promises, "He

shall call upon me, and I will answer him: I will be with him in trouble; I will deliver him, and honour him." Here God precisely declares that He will hear, deliver and honor the believer.

We sing, "What a Friend we have in Jesus," but do we believe it or do we not? When Psalm 27:5 says He is our hiding place in time of trouble, does not God mean what He says?

Further, I am convinced that God takes no delight in the troubles of the ungodly. ". . . for why will ye die?" He cries in Ezekiel 33:11. And in Jeremiah 2:27 the dear Lord says, ". . . for they have turned their back unto me, and not their face: but in the time of their trouble they will say, Arise and save us." Thus we see that God longs for troubled souls to turn to Him for help.

2. Look at and claim His "trouble" promises. We have just seen the promise in Psalm 91 where God promises to be with us in trouble. Also He inspired David to write in Psalm 37:39 that He is our strength in trouble. How wonderful that no matter how weak our troubles make us feel, we find that He furnishes strength at just the right time!

Not only can we call on Him for strength but for comfort. In II Corinthians 7:5, 6 Paul tells us he was troubled on every side so that he was "cast down" but that God comforted him "by the coming of Titus." God helped Paul in his affliction by sending a Christian brother who could help him and give additional comfort.

In other words, others who have been comforted by God are thus qualified to comfort us when we need it. (See II Cor. 1:4.) One word of warning here: We need to be careful that our trust is truly in the Lord and not in even the best of people.

3. It is not enough to know that God can help and that we can refresh ourselves with His promises, but we must learn to WAIT upon Him. In Psalm 27:14 He says, "Wait on the Lord: be of good courage, and he shall strengthen thine

heart: wait, I say, on the Lord."

Waiting is sometimes hard to do but so important, for as Isaiah 40:31 put it, "But they that wait upon the Lord shall renew their strength; they shall mount up with wings as eagles . . . ." God wants us to triumph in our troubles, not be defeated by them, so He tells us that we can soar, even as eagles that mount up above the storm and literally float on the atmosphere of God!

Martha was "troubled about many things," but Jesus said that her sister Mary had "chosen that good part." In other words, Mary was sitting at the feet of Jesus. She had learned to *wait* in the place of learning.

Sometimes God wants us to learn from and get a blessing out of the trouble before He delivers us. David said so in Psalm 46:1: "God is our refuge and strength, a very present help *in* trouble." So our Heavenly Father helps us in as well as out of our troubles.

Nahum 1:7 tells us that our God is "a strong hold in the day of trouble; and he knoweth them that trust in him."

4. Renew your vows to the Lord. Make sure nothing is between your soul and your Saviour. In a time of trial, David cried, "I will go into thy house with burnt-offerings: I will pay thee my vows, Which my lips have uttered, and my mouth hath spoken, when I was in trouble" (Ps. 66:13, 14).

Make a comeback. Rededicate your life and get back into the place of blessing, if God puts His finger on some sore spot in your life.

Note what God says in Psalm 50:14, 15, "Offer unto God thanksgiving; and pay thy vows unto the most High: And call upon me in the day of trouble: I will deliver thee, and thou shalt glorify me."

So God has to sometimes do something IN us before He can do something FOR us.

My days were once such shining things,
  I seemed to feel I wore bright wings.
Came dark I had not known before,
  And folded wings too weak to soar.

Yet somehow spite of grief and care,
  There grew the sense that God was there.
'Twas strange He seemed not near to me
  When hours were filled with laughter free.

Lord, didst Thou clip these wings of mine
  To teach me how to lean on Thine?

5. Know that your troubles will cease. Are not most of the troubles you worried about last year over and done with? In fact, I can hardly remember at all what troubled me a month ago, much less a year ago.

In the opening pages of this book, I mentioned the troubles of several of my acquaintances. The faithful man who had been charged falsely has not only survived, but many blessings have come in the wake of his trouble.

The lovely Christian lady whose husband betrayed her and went off into adultery has experienced God's peace through it all and now is soon to be married to a fine Christian widower who just can't do enough to make her happy. And her Christian friends have stood by her in all her heartaches.

God wonderfully answered prayer for my son and removed the pain from his kidney attack until he could deliver the bus load of youngsters safely back to their homes in Pennsylvania.

The trouble my grandson had with his "lemon" of a car was solved in a most unusual way. He was hit broadside in an accident that was not at all his fault. He was not injured, but the car was a total loss. The insurance company paid for the car, and the one he got for a replacement has turned out to be just what he needed. No more lemon!

We could go on and on. When I see how God has so wonderfully taken care of so many of my troubles, I think of the not-quite-so-bright young man who was always bothered with seemingly little things that greatly troubled him. Once when he was quite disturbed with a problem, he remembered that his pastor had told him to always look in the Bible when he was troubled.

He flipped open his Bible and put his finger down on a verse which began, "And it came to pass. . . ." He knew that didn't make sense (not even to him), so he shut his Bible and opened it again to another passage. Once more he read, "And it came to pass. . . ." He thought, *Well, three times and out—I'll try it again.* So for a third time he shut his Bible, then let it fall open to still a third section of the Book. And once more the verse he put his finger on began, "And it came to pass. . ."!

The young fellow jumped to his feet, rejoicing. "Oh, I see what God is saying. My troubles have not come to stay—they have come to pass!"

Well, it worked for him.

6. Now cast your troubles upon the Lord. In II Corinthians 4:8 Paul declared that he was "troubled on every side, yet not distressed. . . perplexed, but not in despair."

Now this is so important. Our attitude and reaction to trouble has much to do with the outcome. So many times when even little troubles have arisen, I have let myself get "distressed." Many times these distresses are nothing disastrous or fatal—just bothersome. So why get all stressed-out over incidentals? Even with bigger troubles, we are prone to push the panic button and go to pieces instead of facing the problem and getting on to the sometimes simple solution.

If we will but quietly wait on the Lord, He often will show us what to do with the greatest of ease. "When he giveth quietness, who then can make trouble?" (Job 34:29).

When we cry to the Lord in our trouble, He frequently will reply not with some earth-shaking miracle but with a very simple reminder of what we can do to unravel the matter ourselves. ". . .they cried unto the Lord in their trouble, and he delivered them out of their distresses," we read in Psalm 107:6. The trouble is not always immediately gone; but the "distresses" of it can be removed, and His peace can flood our hearts.

"Cast thy burden upon the Lord, and he shall sustain thee: he shall never suffer the righteous to be moved," reads Psalm 55:22. This includes any kind of trouble, for Peter reminds us in I Peter 5:7, "Casting *all* your care upon him; for he careth for you."

The wise King Solomon advises in Proverbs 3:6, "In all thy ways acknowledge him, and he shall direct thy paths." So God often delights to direct us to the exact remedy when we just acknowledge Him about it. How wonderful!

When we do cast our trouble upon Him, it is most expedient that we leave it there and let Him either solve it for us or show us precisely how it is to be done, in His own way and in His own good timing. Remember the beautiful old hymn that goes, "Take your burden to the Lord and *leave* it there."

If I have to hear distressing news, I'd much rather hear it in the daytime, wouldn't you? At night we are prone to take the burden to bed with us. But when we do, then we are not really trusting the Lord to handle the matter.

"What a Friend we have in Jesus, All our sins and griefs to bear!" He is able, and He has never broken any promise spoken.

Second Samuel 22 is a wonderful chapter in which the sweet singer of Israel records his beautiful song of deliverance from many troubles. In the opening verses he has found God to be a rock, a fortress, a deliverer, a shield, a high tower and a refuge. How's that for a start on our troubles?

In verse 4 David is calling on the Lord: "So shall I be saved from mine enemies." In verse 17, when it seemed he was about to be overcome, we have the outcome, "He sent from above, he took me; he drew me out of many waters." In verse 18 he was delivered from strong enemies who hated him. In verse 20 God brought him into a large place.

Thus we see that God can bring us *out* of distresses and into something far better.

What kind of "large place" do we need? a better job? a raise? a new home? a happy marriage? spiritual power? Is some trouble preventing God's best in your life? In verse 31 we learn that "his way is perfect." You can't beat perfection. Now notice in verse 33 that "he maketh my way perfect." The will of God is perfect for us, no matter what He has to allow us to go through to obtain it.

A man stormed out of his home one morning after an exceptionally turbulent clash with his wife at the breakfast table. She had spoken very sharply to him, though she was a professing Christian. He was not yet a believer. As he left the house he exclaimed, "You need a holiday!" (Well, some of us do, don't we?)

This young wife felt that her house of dreams was about to tumble in on her. She went to her knees and turned in her trouble to the Lord, asking Him to forgive her and save her marriage.

That evening when he returned the house was immaculate, the meal was superb, and she looked radiant and beautiful. There was a softness and loveliness about her that caused him to put down his fork and exclaim, "You must have had that holiday!"

She had experienced an inside "holiday" that the poor world knows nothing of.

Where can I go but to the Lord?

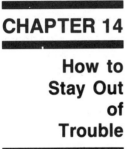

CHAPTER 14

How to Stay Out of Trouble

It is trite but true that prevention is better than cure. What does God teach us about how to stay out of trouble?

David in Psalm 32:7 says, "Thou art my hiding place; thou shalt preserve me from trouble. . . ." But David did not always allow the Lord to do the preserving. In Psalm 34:6 he cries, "This poor man cried, and the Lord heard him, and saved him out of all his troubles."

David could have saved himself so much grief had he simply allowed God to preserve him *from* some of the scrapes he got into.

If only he had gone to battle in II Samuel 11 instead of remaining in the security of the king's house! With time on his hands, he wandered to the rooftop patio in the still of the evening. If only the king had not been there to allow his eyes to wander over to the neighbor's window. But there she was, the beautiful and enchanting Bathsheba "washing herself." If only David had been preserved from feasting his eyes on her and if only she had been bathing where she could not be seen by his eyes.

But that's the way the Devil works. The flesh is weak, the Bible tells us, so we need preserving. "All that is in the world, the lust of the flesh, and the lust of the eyes, and the pride of life, is not of the Father, but is of the world" (I John 2:16). David fell on all three planks of the Devil's platform.

Paul warns, "Wherefore let him that thinketh he standeth take heed lest he fall" (I Cor. 10:12).

Of course sexual temptation is not the only source of trouble for modern saints. There are many other troubles from which we need to be preserved.

Keep in mind that in John 14:1 Jesus said, "Let not your heart be troubled." Just don't let trouble trouble you. Evidently I don't have to LET it happen. If I don't let my heart get troubled, then I can stay out of many troubles my deceitful heart would lead me into.

The truth is, we don't have to have many of our troubles. A great many of mine have been of my own devising.

When as a young lad David was having his difficulties with King Saul, the Bible says, "David behaved himself wisely." Saul was unable to pin anything on David because of the way David "behaved."

So behavior has a lot to do with our being preserved from trouble. The Chinese Christians have a way of saying, "He is reading the Bible and behaving it." In other words, "He has become a Christian and is living the Christian life."

Before we conclude this chapter with some ways to stay out of trouble, please remember that some of our troubles are imaginary. "Most of the troubles people worry over never happen," someone has wisely said. Worry is the advance interest on tomorrow's troubles, many of which never materialize. It is possible to worry oneself into a place of trouble. So how can we be preserved from troubles, both real and imagined?

1. First, make sure of your salvation. By their own admission, a lot of modern-day church members have never truly been born again. It is impossible to live the Christian life if

we are not saved. If you have doubts about it, simply bring those doubts to the Lord. Admit to Him that you are a sinner, tell Him that you do believe that His Son, Jesus Christ, loved you and died in your place on the cross. Then trust Him to save you. Call on Him and tell Him so. Then claim such promises as John 1:12; 3:16; 5:24; 6:37.

It is absolutely imperative that you are saved in order to claim His promises about trouble. In Proverbs 11:8 it is the "righteous" who are delivered from trouble. "But the just shall come out of trouble" in Proverbs 12:13. Righteous and just people are those who have been made righteous (II Cor. 5:21) and justified (Rom. 5:1).

2. *Pray* for daily deliverance from trouble. Jesus taught us to pray, ". . . lead us not into temptation, but deliver us from evil"—a mighty good prayer for the beginning of every day.

"Pray without ceasing" is another command of Scripture. While God knows we cannot go around with our heads bowed and our eyes closed in prayer all the time, it is very possible to live in an attitude of prayer and total dependence upon the Heavenly Father. And we can flash instant prayers all through the day.

When Peter, attempting to walk on the water, cried, 'Help, Lord,' it was not a long, flowery petition, but it caught the attention of the Lord. A longer prayer would have been too late: he was sinking fast.

"Men ought always to pray, and not to faint," Jesus told us in Luke 18:1. So always we should pray about all things. There is no problem or trouble too small to be of interest to our divine Deliverer. If we are fainting, we are not praying—if we pray, we may not faint at all.

Elijah only prayed a sixty-three-word prayer on Mount Carmel after the Baalites had been chanting their prayers all day. But Elijah was the one who had contact with Heaven, and the victory was his. Through prayer his conflict ended.

In your daily routine, stay out of trouble by making prayer as natural as breathing. "If any of you lack wisdom, let him ask of God, that giveth to all men liberally..." (James 1:5).

3. *Avoid* known pitfalls that will lead into trouble. Says Proverbs 15:6, "...in the revenues of the wicked is trouble." One man may never have any temptation to hit the bottle—he just doesn't drink. But he may have to battle lust in his heart—some inclination to the flesh that a sottish old barfly wouldn't even consider.

Hebrews 12:1 speaks of a besetting sin. One woman may have to keep after herself to fight laziness that would lead to trouble in her home. Another, a whiz at housework and cooking, may find that her trouble comes because of her tongue. She says what she thinks—oft without thinking. Each of these two can get into trouble but from two different temptations.

One student may cheat while seated by his or her friend who would never even consider cheating. Envy or jealousy might be something the non-cheater has trouble with.

Proverbs 20:1 says that "Wine is a mocker, strong drink is raging." The individual who would stay out of trouble will avoid all kinds of alcoholic beverages. No total abstainer ever became a drunk.

All of us want warmth and affection. Husbands and wives need one another in every sense of the word. Yet with all of the warnings and promises in the Word of God, millions of marriages are breaking up. The temptation to stray, to play around in sin, seems to be very bold today. Wisdom would dictate, then, that a man carefully avoid the slightest flirtation or carelessness in his daily contact with the opposite sex. If he would avoid trouble in the flesh, he will keep his mind on his work while eagerly anticipating being back with his own wife-lover that night.

Meanwhile, how many women have been tempted to wander and dabble in sin because of the lurid soap operas or the sensual talk shows they watch at home for amusement. If one feeds upon the usual daily fare of TV and music of the rock culture, she is getting her entertainment and inspiration from the lowest possible source.

"Make not provision for the flesh" is the wise command of the Holy Spirit in Romans 13:14. Another good verse for both husband and wife to memorize and keep in mind is, "Abstain from all appearance of evil" (I Thess. 5:22).

People today call an "affair" what God calls wicked, rotten adultery. It always means heartache and misery, if not destruction and death. We reap what we sow. This law has never changed.

4. *Stay* under strong Bible preaching. Early Christians met often for fellowship and for the preaching of the Word of God. Wise Christians still do. We are admonished to "consider one another to provoke unto love and to good works: Not forsaking the assembling of ourselves together." God knows that we need the assembling of ourselves at church on the Lord's day.

There are many hirelings and professional ministers out there today who draw their breath and their salary. There also are many cults and religious weirdos. We should attend church where the Bible is known, loved and proclaimed plainly.

God in II Timothy tells preachers to "Preach the word; be instant in season, out of season; reprove, rebuke, exhort with all longsuffering and doctrine." Sadly, not all preachers obey. But be sure that we need the plain, honest preaching of the Book, including the reproving, the rebuking and the exhortation. The flesh is still weak. In addition, the world still allures and deceives. Add to this the constant bombardment of Satan making war with the saints, and you can be sure we need strong preaching.

Friends and neighbors may wonder why you attend a spiritual church; and you may suffer for righteousness' sake, as Peter suggests in I Peter 3. But he goes on to say that we should not be afraid nor be troubled by this. Instead (to avoid trouble), "... sanctify the Lord God in your hearts: and be ready always to give an answer to every man...." Keep your testimony sharp.

5. *Serve* the Lord by serving others. Second Corinthians 1:4 has taught us that He comforts us in our tribulation that we may be able to comfort them which are in any trouble. As we help others, we strengthen ourselves as well as please the Lord. He tells us to "serve the Lord with gladness" (Ps. 100:2).

Let's lose sight of the enemy in the dust which we stir up serving the Lord. "Be not overcome of evil, but overcome evil with good," Paul counsels in Romans 12:21.

Make a career out of being the very best Christian possible. Win others to Christ. Let your pastor know you are ready to serve. It will thrill him, strengthen you and secure the good favor of the Lord.

6. Maintain a real Christian home. Volumes have been written about marriage, the family and child-rearing. One reason for this is that so many troubles and heartaches originate in the home.

Solomon knew of this and gave many warnings to parents to properly discipline their children if they did not want trouble with them (Prov. 13:24; 19:18; 22:6; 22:15; 23:13, 14; 29:15, 17).

It is never easy to have a godly, happy home, but it is worth it to have such a home at any cost. And it is much easier than mopping up the wreckage.

It is far better to start from the first day of the marriage and never waver.

I have written several booklets on the toddler, the teen, the television, the trials of the family and how to maintain the honeymoon happiness throughout the years. Other able writers have done the same. Time and space do not permit a repeat of all of these truths here.

But standards in deportment, dates, dress, music, reading and television will pay off as long as you live. Character, values and morality will be established long before the children ever become teenagers. This was true in the home in which I grew up, and it proved true in the raising of our own children. I have seen the truth demonstrated in great numbers of homes where I have ministered across America. God has given us a Book to go by. When we depart from it, we can expect trouble.

Stay together. Pray together. Play together. Maintain the prayer and Bible-reading time. Keep your sense of humor. Be consistent, but be fair. Obey God and you'll avoid a lot of heartache. "In the house of the righteous is much treasure: but in the revenues of the wicked is trouble" (Prov. 15:6).

CHAPTER 15

The End of All Trouble

There's trouble ahead for this world. The cup of iniquity surely must be about full. Daniel prophesies "a time of trouble, such as never was since there was a nation even to that same time" (Dan. 12:1). But the rest of the verse assures us "at that time thy people shall be delivered, every one that shall be found written in the book."

Saved people, whose names are written in the Lamb's book of life in Heaven, will escape the Great Tribulation ahead for this Christless, God-hating, Bible-despising generation.

The Tribulation is called also "the time of Jacob's trouble" (Jer. 30:7). The Jews will go through this great time of wrath, but at the end of that time will look upon the Saviour they "pierced" (Zech. 12:10) at the cross; and "all Israel shall be saved: as it is written, There shall come out of Sion [Zion] the Deliverer [Jesus], and shall turn away ungodliness from Jacob" (Rom. 11:26).

"And behold at eveningtide trouble" (Isa. 17:14). Surely evening is coming, and the night of Tribulation will follow for this sordid, sin-laden race.

But the child of God looks for a better day when our troubles will permanently cease. The time is coming when we can say, "The former troubles are forgotten" (Isa. 65:16), for "God shall wipe away all tears from their eyes; and there shall be no more death, neither sorrow, nor crying, neither shall there be any more pain: for the former things are passed away" (Rev. 21:4).

In that day, trouble for the believer will be no more.